Dedication

This devotional is dedicated to my mother, Joyce Fitch. As I ponder on the love of my mother and think back on the way she raised me, all I can think about is how she always just wanted the best for me.

It was her desire for me to be successful one day and to be able to take care of myself. Well, I want to publicly thank her for pushing me into my purpose. Love you, mom!

As a parent, God instructs us to train up our children in the way to go. My mom trained me to never give up and to work hard for what you want.

Teach children in a way that fits their needs, and even when they are old, they will not leave the right path. Proverbs 22:6

Introduction

What you should want most is God's kingdom and doing what he wants you to do. Then he will give you all these other things you need. Matthew 6:33 ERV

Have you ever wondered why you are up early in the morning and can't go back to sleep? And it's not because you have to use the restroom or go to work or someone else? You just find yourself wide awake asking yourself why am I up, why can't I go back to sleep.

Well, could it be that God wants to spend some time with you? Could it be that he wants to talk to you or download some valuable information to you that could help you with a situation? In the Bible, it tells us that Jesus rose early to get away from everyone so He could have some quiet time with God.

God's desire is to talk to us and to keep us safe and protected. If you want to know the heart of God spending quality time with him is one way of learning it. Making God your top priority will benefit your life. He tells us in Matthew 6:33 to seek Him first and everything else will be added unto us. I pray this devotional will help you draw near to ABBA.

Acknowledgments

I first want to thank God for giving me the ability to be able to share His word. I thank him for giving me the fortitude to overcome my fears of believing that I was capable of writing a book and getting it published.

I would like to thank Vision coach Kimberly Springer for listening to the Holy Spirit to do a 30-day challenge that pushed me into action.

I would like to thank Tanya Tenica Patxot for her obedience to hear the vision and encouraged me and others to conqueror fear and every other obstacle that came in our way.

I would like to thank Ms. Judith Taylor for her hard work and dedication to making sure I had everything I needed to complete this assignment. I appreciate her not getting frustrated or irritated when I had to change my launching date a few times.

DAY 1: BEGAINNING YOUR DAY WITH ABBA

Scripture

Matthew 6:33 What you should want most is God's kingdom and doing what he wants you to do. Then he will give you all these other things you need.

How can you apply this today? _____
_____
_____
_____

Today I am grateful for:
_____
_____
_____

NOTES AND REFLECTIONS

DAY 2: BEGINNING YOUR DAY WITH ABBA

Scripture

Romans 8:15 The Spirit that we received is not a spirit that makes us slaves again and causes us to fear. The Spirit that we have makes us God's chosen children. And with that Spirit we cry out, "Abba, Father."

How can you apply this today? _____
_____
_____
_____

Today I am grateful for:
_____
_____
_____

NOTES AND REFLECTIONS

_____

_____

_____

_____

_____

_____

_____

_____

_____

DAY 3: BEGAINNING YOUR DAY WITH ABBA

Scripture

1 Corinthians 2:16 As the Scriptures say, "Who can know what is on the Lord's mind? Who is able to give him advice? But we have been given Christ's way of thinking.

How can you apply this today? _____

_____

_____

_____

Today I am grateful for:

_____

_____

_____

NOTES AND REFLECTIONS

DAY 4: BEGAINNING YOUR DAY WITH ABBA

Scripture

Phillippians 4:13 Christ is one who gives me the strength I need to do whatever I must do.

How can you apply this today? _____
_____
_____
_____

Today I am grateful for:
_____
_____
_____

NOTES AND REFLECTIONS

DAY 5: BEGAINNING YOUR DAY WITH ABBA

Scripture

Romans 8:37 But in all these troubles we have complete victory through God, who has shown his love for us.

How can you apply this today? _____
_____
_____
_____

Today I am grateful for:
_____
_____
_____

NOTES AND REFLECTIONS

DAY 6: BEGAINNING YOUR DAY WITH ABBA

Scripture

Philippians 1:6 I am sure that the good work God began in you will continue until he completes it on the day when Jesus Christ comes again.

How can you apply this today? _____
_____
_____
_____

Today I am grateful for:
_____
_____
_____

NOTES AND REFLECTIONS

DAY 7: BEGAINNING YOUR DAY WITH ABBA

Scripture

John 10:10 A thief comes to steal, kill, and destroy. But I came to give life-life that is full and good.

How can you apply this today? _____

_____

_____

_____

Today I am grateful for:

_____

_____

_____

NOTES AND REFLECTIONS

DAY 8: BEGAINNING YOUR DAY WITH ABBA

Scripture

Philippians 4:19 But my God shall supply all your need according to his riches in glory by Christ Jesus.

How can you apply this today? _____
_____
_____
_____

Today I am grateful for:
_____
_____
_____

NOTES AND REFLECTIONS

DAY 9: BEGAINNING YOUR DAY WITH ABBA

Scripture

2 Corinthians 10:4-5 The weapons we use are not human ones. Our weapons have power from God and can destroy the enemy's strong places. We destroy people's arguments, and we tear down every proud idea that raises itself against the knowledge of God. We also capture every thought and make it give up and obey Christ.

How can you apply this today? _____

_____

_____

_____

Today I am grateful for:

_____

_____

_____

NOTES AND REFLECTIONS

DAY 10: BEGAINNING YOUR DAY WITH ABBA

Scripture

Philippians 4:8 Brother and sisters, continue to think about what is good and worthy of praise. Think about what is true and honorable and right and pure and beautiful and respected .

How can you apply this today? _____

_____

_____

_____

Today I am grateful for:

_____

_____

_____

NOTES AND REFLECTIONS

DAY 11: BEGAINNING YOUR DAY WITH ABBA

Scripture

Matthew 22:37 Jesus answered, Love the Lord your God with all your heart, all your soul, and all your mind.

How can you apply this today? _____
_____
_____
_____

Today I am grateful for:
_____
_____
_____

NOTES AND REFLECTIONS

DAY 12: BEGAINNING YOUR DAY WITH ABBA

Scripture

Jeremiah 29:11 I say this because I know the plans that I have for you. " This message is from the Lord. " I have good plans to give you hope and a good future.

How can you apply this today? _____
_____
_____
_____

Today I am grateful for:
_____
_____
_____

NOTES AND REFLECTIONS

DAY 13: BEGAINNING YOUR DAY WITH ABBA

Scripture

John 14:27 " I leave you peace. It is my own peace I give you. I give you peace in a different way than the world does. So don't be troubled. Don't be afraid.

How can you apply this today? ───────────
──────────────────────────────
──────────────────────────────
──────────────────────────────

Today I am grateful for:

──────────────────────────────
──────────────────────────────
──────────────────────────────

NOTES AND REFLECTIONS

DAY 14: BEGAINNING YOUR DAY WITH ABBA

Scripture

Isaiah 26:3 God, you give true peace to people who depend on you, to those who trust in you.

How can you apply this today? _____
_____
_____
_____

Today I am grateful for:
_____
_____
_____

NOTES AND REFLECTIONS

_____

_____

_____

_____

_____

_____

_____

_____

_____

DAY 15: BEGAINNING YOUR DAY WITH ABBA

Scripture

2 Timothy 1:7 The Spirit God gave us does not make us afraid. His Spirit is a source of power and love and self-control.

How can you apply this today?
_____
_____
_____
_____

Today I am grateful for:
_____
_____
_____

NOTES AND REFLECTIONS

DAY 16: BEGAINNING YOUR DAY WITH ABBA

Scripture

Proverbs 3:5-6 Trust the Lord completely and don't depend on your own knowledge. With every step you take, think about what he wants, and he will help you go the right way.

How can you apply this today? _____
_____
_____
_____

Today I am grateful for:

_____
_____
_____

# NOTES AND REFLECTIONS

DAY 17: BEGAINNING YOUR DAY WITH ABBA

Scripture

1 Peter 2:9 But you are his chosen people, the King's priests. You are a holy nation, people who belong to God He chose you to tell about the wonderful things he has done. He brought you out of the darkness of sin into his wonderful light.

How can you apply this today? _____

_____

_____

_____

Today I am grateful for:

_____

_____

_____

NOTES AND REFLECTIONS

DAY 18: BEGAINNING YOUR DAY WITH ABBA

Scripture

Psalms 90:11 Lord, our God, be kind to us. Make everything we do successful. Yes, make it all successful.

How can you apply this today? _____
_____
_____
_____

Today I am grateful for:

_____
_____
_____

NOTES AND REFLECTIONS

DAY 19: BEGAINNING YOUR DAY WITH ABBA

Scripture

Psalms 37:23 The Lord shows us how we should live, and he is pleased when he sees people living that way.

How can you apply this today? _____

_____

_____

_____

Today I am grateful for:

_____

_____

_____

NOTES AND REFLECTIONS

DAY 20: BEGAINNING YOUR DAY WITH ABBA

Scripture

John 15:13 The greatest love people can show is to die for their friends.

How can you apply this today? _____

_____

_____

_____

Today I am grateful for:

_____

_____

_____

NOTES AND REFLECTIONS

DAY 21: BEGAINNING YOUR DAY WITH ABBA

Scripture

Deuteronomy 28:13 The Lord will make you be like the head, not the tail. You will be on top, not the bottom. This will happen if you listen to the commands of the Lord your God that I tell you today. You must carefully obey these commands.

How can you apply this today? _____

_____

_____

_____

Today I am grateful for:

_____

_____

_____

NOTES AND REFLECTIONS

DAY 22: BEGAINNING YOUR DAY WITH ABBA

Scripture

Psalm 17:8 Protect me like the pupil of your eye. Hide me in the shadow of your wings.

How can you apply this today? _____

_____

_____

_____

Today I am grateful for:

_____

_____

_____

NOTES AND REFLECTIONS

DAY 23: BEGAINNING YOUR DAY WITH ABBA

Scripture

2 Corinthians 10:3-5 We live in this world, but we don't fight our battles in the same way the world does. The weapons we use are not human ones. Our weapons have power from God and can destroy the enemy's strong places. We destroy people's arguments, and we tear down every proud idea that raises itself against the knowledge of God. We also capture every thought and make it give up and obey Christ.

How can you apply this today? _____
_____
_____
_____

Today I am grateful for:

_____
_____
_____

NOTES AND REFLECTIONS

DAY 24: BEGAINNING YOUR DAY WITH ABBA

Scripture

Romans 8:16-18 And the Spirit himself speaks to our spirits and makes us sure that we are God's children, If we are God's children, we will get the blessings God has for his people. He will give us all that he has given Christ. But we must suffer like Christ suffered. Then we will be able to share his glory.

How can you apply this today? _____

_____

_____

_____

Today I am grateful for:

_____

_____

_____

NOTES AND REFLECTIONS

DAY 25: BEGAINNING YOUR DAY WITH ABBA

Scripture

Zephaniah 3: 17 The Lord your God is with you. He is like a powerful soldier. He will save you. He will show how much he loves you and how happy he is with you. He will laugh and be happy about you.

How can you apply this today? _____
_____
_____
_____

Today I am grateful for:

_____
_____
_____

NOTES AND REFLECTIONS

_____

_____

_____

_____

_____

_____

_____

_____

_____

DAY 26: BEGAINNING YOUR DAY WITH ABBA

Scripture

Revelation 3:20 Here I am! I stand at the door and knock. If you hear my voice and open the door, I will come in and eat with you. And you will eat with me.

How can you apply this today? _____

_____

_____

_____

Today I am grateful for:

_____

_____

_____

NOTES AND REFLECTIONS

DAY 27: BEGAINNING YOUR DAY WITH ABBA

Scripture

2 Chronicles 20:15 Jahaziel said, "Listen to me King Jehoshaphat and everyone living in Judah and Jerusalem! The Lord says this to you: 'Don't be afraid or worry about this large army because the battle is not your battle. It is God's battle!

How can you apply this today? _____

_____

_____

_____

Today I am grateful for:

_____

_____

_____

NOTES AND REFLECTIONS

DAY 28: BEGAINNING YOUR DAY WITH ABBA

Scripture

2 Corinthians 5:7 (For we walk by faith, not by sight:).

How can you apply this today? _____
_____
_____
_____

Today I am grateful for:
_____
_____
_____

NOTES AND REFLECTIONS

DAY 29: BEGAINNING YOUR DAY WITH ABBA

Scripture

2 Timothy 1:7 The Spirit God gave us does not make us afraid. His Spirit is a source of power and love and self-control.

How can you apply this today? _____

_____

_____

_____

Today I am grateful for:

_____

_____

_____

NOTES AND REFLECTIONS

DAY 30: BEGAINNING YOUR DAY WITH ABBA

Scripture

Galatians 5:22-23 But the fruit that the Spirit produces in a person's life is love, joy, peace, patience, kindness, goodness, faithfulness, gentleness, and self-control. There is no law against these kinds of things.

How can you apply this today? _____
_____
_____
_____

Today I am grateful for:

_____
_____
_____

NOTES AND REFLECTIONS

www.ingramcontent.com/pod-product-compliance
Lightning Source LLC
Chambersburg PA
CBHW042003150426
43194CB00002B/105